BLUE SHOES

BY THE SAME AUTHOR

A Dream of Maps
A Round House
The Lame Waltzer

BLUE SHOES

MATTHEW SWEENEY

Secker & Warburg
POETRY

First published in Great Britain 1989 by
Martin Secker & Warburg Limited
Michelin House, 81 Fulham Road,
London SW3 6RB

Copyright © Matthew Sweeney 1989

British Library Cataloguing in Publication Data

Sweeney, Matthew, 1952–
  Blue Shoes.
  I. Title
  821'.914
  ISBN 0 436 50844 3

i.m. Raymond Tyner
1924–1988

Printed in Great Britain by
Redwood Burn Ltd, Trowbridge

CONTENTS

ACKNOWLEDGEMENTS

Acknowledgements are due to the following:

Ambit, Aquarius, The Echo Room, Gown, Harry's Hand, Het dwingende verleden: Dertien moderne Ierse dichters, Home and Away: New Poems from the South, Irish Press, Krino, London Magazine, New Statesman, Observer, Orbis, PEN New Poetry 2, Poetry Review, Slightly Soiled, Stand, Times Literary Supplement

'A Couple Waiting' was broadcast on BBC Radio 3.

'At Plath's Grave' makes deliberate use of lines and phrases from the poetry of Sylvia Plath.

THE COLD

After the all-hours drinking bout,
and the punchless acrimony,
he set off for the sea, on foot,
a good mile in the wind,
past zigzag lines of parked cars
and the disco din, past streetlights,
though if he'd needed light
the stars would have done –
down to the beach he wobbled,
a beercan in both pockets,
to sit on a rock and drink,
and think of his marriage,
and when both cans were empty
he removed his shoes
to walk unsteadily into the sea
and make for Iceland,
but the Atlantic sent him home again,
not a corpse, not a ghost,
to waken his wife
and complain of the cold.

THE SEA AT POLLAN

Annie Denny
who lived in the house above the sea,
a scant half-mile down from me,
could read the clouds
and predict a drowning,

not that there were many
though once when I was six or seven
a procession of men and women
snaked uphill –
I saw it from my room

and at its head
four men carried on an old door
a brother they'd lost a week before
who'd bobbed to land
at the base of a cliff,

the same cliff
pups and kittens were thrown from,
there being no way home –
except when a door
was lowered on ropes.

From the top
on a blue morning you can see Scotland
and pick the best mushrooms in Ireland,
then hit the road
at Annie's house

though she's long gone
and the barbed wire guarding the field
is now loose enough to yield
when you climb over
with a bag of mushrooms.

Down the road
come German campers in twos and threes
to their orange tents by the sea
on the ex-golfcourse
that earlier still

in neutral days
saw a Messerschmidt forced to land
by its empty tank, and farmers surround
it with pitchforks
till the army came.

It's quieter now
in Pollan. At night the cars come
and sit there with their radios on
at a country station
that's good for love

and one night
a friend and I crept, cursing, past
carrying between us a baby bath
three-quarters filled
with the sea,

fronds and all,
in a beer-inspired attempt to keep
two lobsters alive – we'd bought cheap
from a fisherman
after we'd eaten.

DOG ON A CHAIN

This red setter was another red setter
who ran with his red tongue out
down the road, over fields and sand
into the sea; who came out shaking water
and loped by himself the long way home,
then lay on pebbles in the sun.
But after the car from over the border
mashed his hip, he lay on a rug
then limped for years, till a lump
grew on him, and the vet brought a gun.

In this second life he is lithe again
and doesn't howl at the chapel bell.
He howls at his long chain instead
that keeps him from the car-filled road,
and from the sheep and cattle
and their farmers who threaten guns.
But the next time he slips the chain
he'll run with his red tongue out
down the road, over fields and sand
into the freezing, gull-cluttered sea.

THE BORDER

Twenty miles south is the North
where I was booked in to be born –
a nursing home in a Derry suburb,
but my mother went on playing bridge
and never made it past the border.

Fireworks, coconuts and kippers
came over later, and stones of butter
packed under the Volks's back seat,
away from the confiscating urge
of the Customs man in his warm hut.

It wasn't butter the B Specials wanted
when their bullets skimmed our bumper –
we'd missed their waved red light,
so shouts interrogated us
while a torch-beam frisked the car.

These nights headlights go off
as you cross the border, and rifles
in soldiers' hands motion you to stop
outside the sandbagged checkpoint
that gave some local mason work.

NORTH

The drone of a plane or a lawnmower
niggles the early evening air
as I look through lace curtains to where
our lane ends and the road begins –
the road that goes a half-mile north
or three hundred miles south,
past stations, ports and airports.
North, we find a curved, empty beach.

Sometimes I stand at the sea's edge
and watch for ships passing, but either
they travel by night or keep to the south
for nothing crawls across the horizon –
not even the hulk of the Laurentic
risen from the sea-bed, and certainly not
the liner, whose lifeboat is heading
my way, to whisk me elsewhere.

DIGESTING CRAB CLAWS

'Don't fall apart on me tonight . . .'
The tape's up loud and Dylan's back
from the Crusades, and we sit
half a mile from the frothed Atlantic,
digesting a bucket of crab claws
as the sea wind tests the putty.
An hour now and we haven't stirred
from this table, except to change
the tape, and feed the range
that eats turf like a generator
though its back boiler is holed.
And I pulled on the anorak
to go for turf, past the line
where a blue flag of jeans
makes the pegs earn their keep,
and back inside, I spoke
of slates that scythed down,
and of snapped-off branches.
No-one listened. They stared out
at the would-be mountain opposite,
as if someone scuttled there
wearing red, past the houses,
then their upwardly errant sheep,
to stand, hunched, on the ridge
with the cairn and the tv booster
barely visible to us below.

THE CRAB ROCK

Even in a bad summer the tide goes out
till the crab rock is revealed,
though the crabs like sun, like to climb there
and lie, as if dead, or lazily scuttle
among themselves, over weed and mussels.

Enough of their dead litter the beach
on the approach to the rock, waiting for water
to move them, out where no dog
or gull can poke them, where they'll dissolve.
They are back before the others know it.

The crab rock is never embedded in sand,
always those yards for us to wade through,
then the walk through edible claws
on bare edible toes. There are many crabs,
they are home, they are armoured.

I bet they leave when the sea covers,
though it's seldom deep there. A man could stand
all night and keep his head in air.
There are worse pastimes. Rain wouldn't matter.
The crabs would keep their distance.

WHERE FISHERMEN CAN'T SWIM

Back there where fishermen can't swim,
where the ice-age coast of Donegal
leaves rocks among the waves,
a lobster-boat cast off, whose engine
croaked before the rocks were by.
The youngest in the crew leapt out
onto a rock to push the boat away,
then laughed when he couldn't jump back.
But exactly when did he realise
that the boat would float no nearer;
that all those pulls on the engine cord
would yield no shudders; that no rope
or lifebelt existed to be thrown;
that those flares were lost in cloud;
that the radio would bring a copter
an hour later? He had forty minutes –
to cling while the waves attacked,
to feel the rock gradually submerge.
And they had forty minutes of watching,
shouting into the radio, till he cried
out, sank from view, and stayed there.

THE LIGHTHOUSE KEEPER'S SON

got arrested
as he wobbled home
on a lightless bicycle
after a late drink,
and he asked the cop
if the pockmarked moon
wasn't light enough
not to mention the Plough's
seven stars,
and his dad's beam
igniting the road
twice a minute,
then searching the sea
the umpteenth time
for nothing

A COUPLE WAITING

Leaving the door of the whitewashed house ajar
the man runs to the top of the hill
where he shields his eyes from the evening sun
and scans the sea. Behind him, a woman
holds a curtain back, but when he turns
and shakes his head, she lets the curtain fall.
She goes to the mirror beneath the flag
where she searches her face for signs of
the change her body tells her has begun.
The man shuts the door and sits at the table
where a chicken's bones are spread on two plates.
He thinks of his friends on the Atlantic,
coming up the western coast, laden
with well-wrapped bundles for his stable
that no horse uses. He thinks of his country,
and how his friends and he, with the help
of those bundles, would begin to set it right.
He calls the woman over and feels her stomach,
then asks why she thinks the boat is late.
Like him, she's harassed by an image –
the boat, searchlit, in French or Spanish waters,
guns pointed, a mouth at a megaphone.
Like him, she does not voice her mind,
instead sends him to the hill once more
in the dying light, to watch the red sun
sink in the water that's otherwise bare,
while she sits in the dark room, thinking
of the country their child will grow up in.

A DAYDREAM AHEAD

The car you bought
stays white that first Spring,
or it does in my imagining
as I daydream ahead
and I am not there.

You step out
to a familiar petrol pump
(though new to me), plump
with the third child
you said you wanted.

The car is a make
I do not recognise
though I can tell by its size
how much you're earning
or your new man is.

Your hair is short
and it suits. You look good,
the few years have made
no difference.
You like life now.

Back in the car
you speed along a coast
that looks like the West
of Ireland.
You have gone home.

You come to a drive,
gravel sprays beneath you.
Your bungalow is new,
with portholes
and bay windows.

I sit at my window
whose net curtain blurs
a coloured line of cars
at parking-meters
beneath streetlights.

CALAIS

Even the playground is empty,
the sun polishing the yellow and blue
of the domed climbing-frame,
taxis and cars parked at home –
perhaps it's a day for Calais,
leaving by coach early,
the hovercraft, the seasick,
the late, clinking arrival back.

But who's this back so soon,
wheeling her case alone
up the concrete path, waiting
at the lift door, stretching
her back, till she disappears
up to whichever floor
her empty flat is on?
How long has she been gone?

Weeks, at least, I'd say.
Perhaps she'd meant to stay
a lifetime, but relented –
and now, dutyfree-scented,
she unpacks, undresses
while the shower hisses
to the right temperature,
and in the ghosting mirror

she glimpses her face
that's older than the face
he remembers, but kinder too,
ready to have a go
at loving him again,
hoping he feels the same,
then she soaps the sweat away,
and the dust from here to Calais.

FOR THE LIVING

It was like this:

my grandmother, ten years dead,
sitting by the range;
me on the sofa with a new girl,
arm around her neck,
while up and down the stairs
traipsed friends I'd kept up with
and friends I'd forgotten.

My grandmother was laughing
with me and my girl,
applauding our cuddles,
and the ten years hadn't shaved
a single slice
from her plump cheeks,
or let the bones push through.

I left her there,
lady from the cemetery.

Knew she'd pray for me.

THE WOMEN

The women are lighting fires
and snapping drunks –
their own drunks, men
whose eyes will be closed
on the prints that come back
from the chemist; men
seen past a whisky bottle
on the table, drinking
from delft eggcups
beneath pictures of the dead.

The women are drinking too,
off-camera – till a child
grabs the camera
and snaps them, their laughs,
their glasses raised,
their mock dances to music
on the wireless; and the men
with their eggcups still,
deep in chairs, watching.
And the child wondering.

THE SHADOW HOME

As his daughter watches from the doorway
she can't realise how exactly
she has got him right – how each time
he carries his kitbag to the bus
he will end his journey at another house
where another daughter will wait for him.
And another wife will embrace him,
as her mother did just now,
and all three will go inside.
What she doesn't know, his daughter, is where –
some corner of Connecticut,
some Atlantic island – there are no leads,
and she would never ask.
And does her shadow-sister look like her?
Is she blonde, is her mother blonde,
do they speak English, has her father
hidden a language for years?
And does he take his other daughter
on long walks through the pines,
and tell her about his travels,
about the people he's met, about himself?
There is so much about her father
she does not know, and so little time
between his absences to learn it.
Does her shadow-sister know about her,
or does she begin to suspect?
Which of the two is the shadow home?

BOY WITH A ROD

Along the bank of a river,
past resting swans,
a boy with a rod is running –
he must be fifteen
and the rod must be fifteen feet,
and the line and hook
are switching the air,
scarcely avoiding branches,
scattering oncomers,
till, with a laugh, he reaches
his stationary friend
whose hook waits in the water.

And, watching from the patio
of a still-empty pub,
between sips of ale,
a new-to-eachother
man and woman see
the boy flick his line
till it half-disappears,
and settle his boots
to wait all evening,
then perhaps let the fish go –
just as the man and woman
may never meet again.

ON MY OWN

I stop, in my tracksuit, on a sleeper.
I lay my ear to the line
and if I hear a hum, slide
down the embankment, and wait
among the coke-cans and beetles
till the express shakes by.
I think of last week, and McArdle
headless when the train had gone.
I scramble up to the tracks
that are blankly silver, and the sea
comes in view, and the young forest,
and the cross-country race I abandoned,
and my school's water tower – and I
head towards Dublin on my own.

HITCHHIKING

The role of sex is exaggerated –
though a blonde at a motorway slip-road
will jump the queue. Best to pair off,
then hide while she thumbs alone.
Watch for knives beneath the dashboard
and sullen men. Jeeps are alright,
especially if a map of the world
adorns the bonnet, and the driver says
he's back from a three-year trip
round the globe, and he takes you
on a tour of the Mâcon villages
to sample the wines, then home
to his château and Maman, and a bed.
Take care to keep awake in cars,
otherwise you'll double back
100 kilometres, cursing your Italian,
and at night, on the French border,
get in with a Yugoslav, bound for Paris
but crazy with the toothache,
who asks if you're a dentist,
then swigs his Slivovitch again.
It helps to have French ancestors
and enough of the lingo to relay this.
It helps to be an actor, and carry
a red towel for bullfight towns,
and a thick felt-tip for signs
on the backs of maps, names of cities
you've read about, and '1 kilometre'
for occasions you're stuck.
Watch out for Frankfurt cops
who shunt you on the autobahn,
then book you for the privilege,
and you're stranded there till a kid

shows a red breakdown triangle,
then beckons you to run.
Be prepared to climb into anything
from a Daimler to a knacker's truck
whose stench makes you puke
and sends kids scurrying in towns.
Draw the line, perhaps, at a hearse.

THE COLOUR OF TELEPHONES

What colour is your telephone?
Is it blue, like mine –
blue in a blue-painted room
where the sun, at dawn,
comes down the stairs
from the roof-garden?
The colour is more important
than you may realise. Did you
send back a beige phone,
like I did, or is beige
your colour, your everyday?
After the maze of connection,
through subterranean tunnels,
via satellites,
it's essential to visualise
the person you speak to,
not just fix on a voice,
and the colour of the receiver
held to a mouth and ear
is a necessary detail,
as necessary as hairstyle.
You should give it to friends
when you give the number,
should keep it from strangers.
When you inherit a phone,
change the colour –
it's your personality, your secret,
a secret you should share.

THE U-BOAT

I am floating by the wrecked U-boat,
naked as a dolphin in the August sun.
I've got away, again, from everyone.
I've moored my raft to the periscope
that stays underwater. On it I keep
my shorts and shoes, and coca-cola,
and a Bavarian girly magazine.
I've become so at-home in the ocean
that I think I must someday drown.
Miles away, on the edge of my hometown,
twin cooling towers fork the sky
where an airship phuts, selling beer.
No-one knows the U-boat is here –
no boats approach these rocks,
no swimmers advance. I don't advertise.
I dive to the conning-tower and enter.
Bubbles speed behind me, above me,
but I am fast. I slide past my friend
the skeleton, until my breath runs low,
then I hit the surface he saw long ago
but never quite saw in the end.

LEAVING THE SURFACE

Consider it probable
that today, on some blue-skied atoll,
a team of men are busy,
naked to the waist, and sweaty,
lowering bundles
of perspex and fibreglass
to frogmen builders,
at it for years,
constructing a fabulous city
no satellite will see,
whose handpicked, future citizens
watch no screens
nor read no papers –
they include brewers and bakers
but no military –
already they can see
the identikit homes
they'll dive to when the call comes,
leaving for looters
address-books and furniture,
leaving bills unpaid,
abandoning their dead,
keeping only the heat
from the piped, filtered sunlight,
leaving the surface
to its own devices.

A POSTCARD OF A HANGING

for Padraig Rooney

I sent you a postcard of a hanging,
the first one I attended, not thinking
I'd like it, or even stand it, as you
must have loathed my postcard too
till you realised it must be a trick,
a decadent, oriental gimmick
to put liberals off their breakfast
of an egg, toast, jam and the rest.

I imagine your laughs then, the card
propped against the milk, as you read
again how I thrived in the East –
every meal a ginger and chilli feast;
the girls; the boys . . .; how vibrant
the hours and how little I spent.
And you believed it, you knew
that all my varied antics were true.

And you turned to the picture again,
a colour print – a gallows, two men,
one hooded, one holding a noose
of whitest rope, for the moment loose,
and low in the foreground, a crowd
of men mainly, silently loud,
all eastern, except for two or three –
one of whom, if you look closely, is me.

DREDGING THE LAKE

While it rained they dredged the lake again.
There was no-one about, no-one watching –
that was what they thought. They were wrong.
They thought they were safe, mid-morning
before term began, in a sea-fall of rain.
They forgot there are folk who don't belong.

They had one hour, with a boat and a van
with a winch on top. They worked fast –
five of them, all men with hoods up
and waders to the crotch. Pros to the last,
they hunted for something – a drowned pup,
the bloated, eyeless body of a man?

Whatever it was they bumped off without it
over grass, with the boat winched high –
though they did bunch together, I recall,
at the water's edge. Or do I trust an eye
that the rain kept indoors, and that later lit
on a jogger in red who kept it in thrall?

THE STATUES

I stared through the bay window
past a fly sunning itself
as it listened to birdsong.
On the left, a long-jump away,
stood a magnolia in flower,
shedding its leaves in May.
On the right, a pink rhododendron
was being cased by a bee
while ahead, in the shelter
of a medieval larch,
in a diminutive sentry-box
stood Joseph and the Infant
amid an audience of bushes.
I stared past the greenhouse
and the heaped pots of paint.
Behind me were thirty doors
(if you count the dumb-waiter),
all in this small house,
some opening nowhere,
some showing ex-classrooms
with the desks intact,
awaiting exams; some locked
or ushering one into armchairs
arranged in a ring
next door to the kitchen –
and everywhere, statues
watching over nobody
in those rooms, those corridors,
Mary, the Boy, the Man,
the Saints and the Blesseds,
conspiring in an almost-whisper
to remind of the decades
where nuns' skirts were long
and there were queues to fill them.

THE HAUNT OF THE NIGHT-OWL

At midnight the hum of the telly goes on
when the voices are abed. I hear it
from my bed, one floor above, till you
shuffle over to fiddle the knobs, hoping
for other voices, anything still awake.
Your favourites are snooker and crime
but tonight you switch off, and your voice
slips through my floor like a gruff ghost,
waking the old woman on the mattress
next to yours in that mess of a room
where the radiators stay on in summer
ever since your TB, her diabetes,
and where the windows stay closed.
All night you mutter about nothing,
and none of it good, making sure
she hears you (you reach me too . . .),
breaking out into roars, sometimes,
when she shits, then rolls, in the bed.
You're not one for baths, much, yourself.
I can sniff when you've been downstairs
with your two carrier bags for basics –
bread, milk, clanking bottles of beer;
to answer the door or handle our mail.
Each morning a black nurse visits –
how this bugs you, but nowadays
you admit her, you've been warned
and you're getting on – and twice weekly
an ambulance cools outside, as two men
carry your woman down in a wheelchair
and away, to return her in hours.
Often when they get here, you're out,
or asleep, grabbing rest for the night.

OMELETTES

A mattress stands on its side
with a cat asleep on top.
Behind it, the musty curtains
admit a chunk of sunlight,
while before it, a man of 70
lies, in his clothes, in a bed
and waits for the ambulance.
A tin with roll-up butts,
two cups, and a pils can
are on the floor; the smell
is of urine and damp wallpaper.
He complains of the pain
in his bandaged arm and knee,
and talks to the other bed
whose owner now is dead,
two weeks back, and looks
at me. He speaks of the hospital,
how he knows the area well –
how he lived and worked there,
a second chef in a defunct hotel,
eight years, and he asks me
how many omelettes there are,
then answers, hundreds,
and tells me the best he saw
was when he took treacle
in place of oil, and the first chef
got the omelette off intact
and he doesn't know how he did.

MAY 1, 1987

for Sarah Maguire

Someone is tinkering with the phone –
for minutes a half-ring has fluttered
into the kitchen; then it rings
and I pick up a Middle European voice,
slow, inaudible, another wrong number.

I keep the windows on one side closed –
it's the lime-dust from the site.
A year back it was Chernobyl.
A year back I had a position,
two homes, and good hypochondria.

The old man, my neighbour, is gone –
his hospital prediction came true.
My publisher is under the Receiver.
I peel an overripe banana,
hoping it is good for a hangover.

THE MAN WITH THE BUDGIE
ON HIS BACK

The man with the budgie on his back
walks, stooped, to the bar
and brings back a tray of beers.
His movements are slow, as if
he fears the budgie might leave,
but the budgie is fixed to his back
like it grew there. The man's friends,
two girls and a man, are laughing
but they are not 'budgie people'.
They approach other drinkers, passers-by,
offering the blue budgie as a gift
but the most they get is a smile.
The man takes the budgie to the loo,
then brings it back again. Nowhere
is there irritation on his face.
The budgie knows how to choose,
and sits there, on the checked shirt
that it likes so much, looking round
at more people than it's seen before,
most of them looking its way.
The man's friends want to leave.
They head off down the street
slowly, with the man still stooped
and the budgie in place,
as if they'll always be this way.

ELECTRIC CARS

Imagine – allover – the purr of electric cars!
No need for zebras, all hurries abolished –
except for the ambulance, which, silent as a hearse,
whips along its own track, high overhead.
And at night, the electric re-creation of gaslamps
yellowing the smoke-free air, neon banned
or shunted indoors, the headlights filtered.
Imagine being mobile in that kind of city!

Today I bustled through this kind of city,
my Wednesday morning lap from home to home,
and the cars followed me, braking at corners,
accelerating again, the slush of their wheels
through landed drizzle forcing the engines louder,
the horns more frequent. But near Kings Cross,
outside where Lenin lived, I met an electric car –
a milk van – and papers ablaze in a paint can.

TO THE BUILDING TRADE

Here's to the building trade,
to the renovations and facelifts,
the fake Victorian façades;
to the dust-muffled din
that stops on Sundays;
to the men that make it,
especially one from Dalston
who, after a pint or two
and a ploughman's, fell –
but the scaffolding stayed up
till the flats were clean.
Here's to the offduty cabbie
in the first-floor kitchen
who saw him splatter
on the pavement; to the mate
with the trowel, staring down,
his question unanswered;
to the rent increase
and the officer who set it.
Here's to the young widow
whose home's in this city
where migrant scaffolding,
wherever she moves,
will find her walls sometime.

NO ANSWER

A woman in curlers sits by a phone,
a blue phone to a white house.
All morning while the friseur pattered
she catalogued her phrases
but all morning the big chief was out.
She has so much to tell him –
about poverty-deterrents, juggled figures,
a tax that's a new contraceptive –
that an airlift might be called for,
a Harrier from the South Atlantic,
taking off and landing in the dark.
She pushbuttons again: an empty ring,
where can the guy be? The friseur
is back to liberate the tresses
she will flaunt at a flashlit lunch,
after the microphones and biros
and the midge-drone of their owners.
She swallows; why are kippers bony
in this nuclear age, and why does
tannin not dissolve the bones away?
A mirror tours her head
till dismissed by a nod. It'll do.
She connects, then hangs up again.
The damn fool is never home.
Spends his life making dates
with bald, hatted men, on icebergs.
Why don't they meet on the moon?

SYMMETRY

Gentlemen, you will please wear a tie
while peeing. And in the criss-cross corridors
you will pass without touching,
as you journey to and from the dining-room
under the portraits of Prime Ministers,
(except for the woman). You will sit
equally spaced apart, four facing four,
with one (each of you in turn) facing me
down the long, driftwood table.
While eating, you needn't call me Sir.

Two legs of lamb must be carved
simultaneously. Decide among yourselves.
And eat as much or as little as you like
but eat the same. Your weights
must match at the end as at the start;
must be half of mine. And no glass
can go empty of blood-red wine
till the clock-hands cross at midnight
when I will retire. Leaving nine.
Gentlemen, you will please set that right.

PINK MILK

When the goats ate the red carnations
and the next morning's milk was pink,
the abbot loved it, demanded more

but the monks loved their flower-garden
and turned to cochineal, to crushed ants,
to paprika, all stirred in milk

to no avail – the perfume was gone
and the abbot grumpy, so carnations
were sacrificed to rampant goats

whose beards jigged as they chewed,
who looked up at the watching monks
while the abbot watched from a window

and in the kitchen, a leg of pork
thawed on a hook from the ceiling,
and blood dripped into a milk-jug.

HOW WITCHES WENT INVISIBLE

They boiled a black cat alive,
boiled it till the bones loosened,
took these singly in their teeth,
then stood before a mirror
till one bone defied reflection.

With this they were grinning winds
whooshing through the alleys,
masturbating in the marketplaces,
making pigs' heads float,
heading for home with fresh roots
and black cats at their seethrough feet.

THE QUEUE

At dusk I took a doubledecker to the queue
that I knew would be there already.
I brought with me my sleeping-bag –
it was a warm evening – also a book,
salt beef on rye, a naggin of whisky,
and my walkman primed with Tom Waits.

I know not everyone likes Tom Waits
but I do. I was right about the queue
(one extra reason for the whisky!) –
there must have been up to twenty already.
I unrolled my sleeping-bag
and wriggled in, then opened up my book.

I suppose I should tell you about that book.
It's one of my favourites: *The Weight
of a Corpse is Varied*. The sleeping-bag
was duck-down and the best in the queue
that had grown behind me already.
I took a shuddery swig from the whisky.

Would I, I thought, be mugged for my whisky?
Perhaps I'd brought the wrong choice of book
when thoughts like this already
were in my head. We had a long wait
till 9 a.m., and with this size of queue,
might end up with nothing. As sleep in a bag

goes I had a good night in that sleeping-bag.
I slept for an hour at least. The whisky
lasted well. I was the envy of the queue
as I slid it to my lips, behind the book,
with the crackly seepage of Tom Waits
in the streetlit air. Then it was dawn already

and I watched my queue-mates all ready
themselves – some left their sleeping-bags
to walk around, forgetting the wait
they still had. I finished the whisky
and lay on, chortling at my book,
by this stage in the vanguard of the queue.

You must be wondering about this queue.
If I said each of you would be ready
to join it, with or without a book,
(most had none, though they had sleeping-bags)
you'd say I was too long on the whisky,
like that stubbled croaker, Tom Waits.

But I'll say more. I'll say this queue's for books,
for sleeping-bags, for tapes of Tom Waits,
for whisky, for anything, and you're in it already.

THE ALIBI

Turning his telescope on the moon
Magnus considers his alibi –
himself and Sarah in Regent's Park
stuffing the squirrels with nuts
till one twister bit his thumb.

Then home with a bloodied shirt
to Maisie with her throat cut,
stretched beneath the piano.
And his name on the house-deeds
along with hers, and Sarah

on the neighbours' tongues for weeks.
So up to the roof he staggers
to get some air, focussing
the telescope without thinking,
till the moon is there, almost full.

HER SONG

Singing, she pedalled over the moonlit bridge.
Did the trout in the river listen
to her alto warble, or did the words
go unheard to the lowest stars?
Her own words, wedded impromptu
to the theme-tune from *Doctor Zhivago* –
words that detectives in bushes
would relish, but they were still in bed.

And already behind her, the moon was outdone
by the flames in the thatch, showing
the whitewash going brown, then black,
the pony rearing at his rope,
the Saab locked in the yard,
and no-one in burning pyjamas
framed for a second in the doorway.
Her song was telling the trout why.

FLYING MACHINES

Waking to the sight of a windsock
on a deserted airfield, I inquire
and learn that men and women
jump from planes here, or loop
their loops, even into the ground.
I'm told that one rookie landed
on another taking off. I consider
Heathrow with my old fervour.
I travel by train to the west
where I'm brought on a windy walk
up a high path, among trees.
Far off, the Severn sprawls
as if it had no sea. And above me's
a glider, white and skull-frail,
audible above the wind! Skimming
the tree-tops metres from my head.
A model plane with someone inside.
And I think of the kits I bought
in Derry, then glued by numbers –
Spitfires, and Messerschmidts,
Hurricanes, and Stukas; the hours
I spent on these, and on thoughts
of landing in the local bay
in my own flying boat, ferrying
friends to the party on the island –
me, who needs brandy to walk
towards a smiling hostess
up the gangway of a DC 10.

THE MONK'S WATCH

I flew out on the night of a January full moon.
As we rose above Heathrow I saw it through glass –
I can tell you it startled me. I continued to watch
it as London shrank, anything to take
my mind off statistics of disintegrating planes.
Then I noticed my companion was a monk.

Whose seat better to adjoin than a monk's
in case we should fall! He was bald as the moon
and stood out among the tenants of that plane
as surely as a species behind glass.
I threw him a glance as he struggled to take
something from his pocket. He watched me watch

and flicked me a grin. 'If you wish to watch
me hunt in my pocket, fine. A monk
is an object of curiosity, it seems. Otherwise take
your eyes away and turn them on the moon,
growing bigger by the moment through the glass,
in case it should collide with this plane.'

I was the most shocked punter on that plane!
A caustic padré indeed! I glanced at my watch
and summoned the burnished hostess for a glass
of Bushmills which I banged on my table. The monk
sniffed, then stared across me at the moon
with as much curiosity as that ball could take.

'I wonder how much gelignite it would take
to make smithereens of that?' he murmured. The plane
was decidedly less safe when I imagined the moon
in fragments, especially when he began to watch
my expression, as I recalled the monks
who'd taught me years ago. I refilled my glass

and turned to see it reflected in the glass
of the window, wondering what he'd take
from the pocket of that habit I thought monks
had abandoned. At that the plane
tilted viciously, losing us the moon,
and the monk's hand appeared with a fob watch.

The moon came back. We got on fine, that monk
and I, downed glasses together, drowned the plane
in laughter, and in Belfast that watch was mine to take.

THE VICTORIAN CEMETERY
AT HIGHGATE

Catacombs, vaults, tombs, massive coffins –
the dead must enjoy such space

plus the peace of undergrowth around them
and the limit on their ruly population

but not, surely, this mound of wreaths,
this spoor of an interloper –

a French chef who bivouacked in ice
while his francs converted and found

a vault empty where none should be,
but the dead don't get to sign petitions

so flesh lies surrounded by bones
and at night God alone knows what happens.

AT PLATH'S GRAVE

She would rather be horizontal, she wrote –
then the trees would touch her, the flowers have time for her.
Well, she got grass and a single yellow rose
with one petal withered and a dead bee inside.
And the grave obscure in an overflow field
with that newer surname chipped off again
leaving a blacker black on the upright marble.

It took eye-flits and a mazy search to find it
and as I was leaving a new friend came
to stand with me above her, quoting her lines
in that knocking tone of recent teenagers.
I heard him out and glanced down, then took him
by the arm through the graves to a pub
where we shot pool under a green-shaded lamp.

2

She had one too many dimensions to enter.
When it thundered she hid under a flat stone.
It is more natural to her lying down.
She is at home here among the dead heads,
the head-stone quiet, jostled by nothing.
She is nobody; she has nothing to do with explosions.
Over her bones the clouds go; they mollify the bald moon.

THE COFFIN SHOP

In the coffin shop everyone is busy,
there are three hands at every phone.
They still approach if you're in a hurry
– they recognise the recently alone,
and drop the chatter to be beside you
in white suits, with mauve bow-ties.
Their eyes are expressive as pandas
who have mastered maths. Their talk
swings to holidays in the country
where the corpse is headed, at expense,
a detail they arrange, while you look
the coffins over, to their commentary
of how each was made, and the lead
that lines this one, to deter invaders,
and the gold on that one, and the wood.
They poke the velvet cushions for the head,
they stand back and turn to face you
– you'd hardly decline if you could.

MACKIE

Remember Mackie, the undertaker's apprentice?
How he'd stand at the bar, never sit,
and tell us how he hated Mondays.
How the first week he worked there
he couldn't sleep on his back –
he imagined the dark in those boxes he varnished,
and how someone like him would nail together his.
How we'd look at each other and shake the head,
sliding him a small one as we left
to continue in the pub down the street.
How we suggested college, or the priesthood.
How we talked about premonitions
when the news came in – the one
piece of Sputnik debris that fell locally
fell on his head, one midnight
when he'd stayed on afterhours.
How we took to the drink for weeks.
How we avoided his punk successor.
How we agreed he knew all about it now.

A DIARY OF SYMPTOMS

For weeks I've kept a diary of my symptoms
for my eyes alone. It lies in the drawer
with the carbon and the blank paper, as if
it belonged there. I keep the poems apart.
At any waking time I bring it out
and add the latest news from the body.

I'm trying to be helpful to my doctors.
I'll show them I, too, am professional,
and maybe we'll win. I don't demand much –
just health. I'm not hunting my youth
or a sprinter's fitness, or a priest's looks.
I just want to be here to write some books.

TUBE RIDE TO MARTHA'S

Before the sirens started, he was late –
late for a dinner at his woman's,
but he'd managed to find a good Rioja
and an excellent excuse: his cat
had burned her tail in the toaster
(this was true) and he'd brought her
to the vet and back in a cab.
He thought about a third cab to Martha's
but funds were low, and the tube ride
was four stops, a half hour with the walks.
He had a thriller in his carrier-bag,
a Ross McDonald, long out of print,
which he opened on the escalator, wanting
it finished tonight. When the smoke came
he hardly noticed, till the black guard
tried to hustle everyone upstairs,
and trains rushed by, without stopping,
and people pushed and screamed.
As the smoke got thicker and blacker
with flames growing fast, he realised
it was over, almost before it had begun.

BLUE SHOES

I see that day's non-headlines, as he did
    though they're smoky now –
a prince at playschool, a brat's bethrothal.
Some days they rob the gossip entries
    in lieu of disasters.
    They missed his later.

The weather inch reads more like Sicily
    than England. I see him
hurrying towards the train, his hand
raised to his eyes, the sunglasses at home.
    I have his notes here,
    the last of any consequence.

All the women, it seems, wore blue shoes
    in keeping with the morning.
He played with patterns, with omens
he deciphered later. That particular day
    it was blue shoes
    for want of any better.

I see him with a letter and xeroxed map
    leaving the station.
He is sucking mints, perhaps hungover.
At the school gates he checks his flies.
    He goes in the office,
    is lost from sight.

Did they know the strain of these visits?
    Did the kids care?
It was a long day, but not outlandish.
In his honour they had lunch in a pub.
    On another day
    it would have relaxed him.

He was chauffeured to the train in the end,
    an overwound watch.
He queued at a phone, his heart chugging.
A woman was speaking, a man waiting –
    the woman, he wrote,
    wore blue shoes.

Hard for me in this library to imagine
    that home journey,
the mounting pain in his mind and chest,
the prison of that train in motion.
    All I know is
    he thought he was dead.

And got off at a suburban station
    to ride in an ambulance
through all the jams of South London
to nurses and a narrow bed with wheels
    and electric wires
    on feet, wrists and heart.

I am reading over his own description
    of that evening –
how later, at home, he imagined
he'd got away with it, and drank.
    He got away
    for the time being.

For years, even, but what does it matter –
    he never forgot
that day of the interrupted train,
the only time in his life, late sun
    and pretty women
    wearing blue shoes.